Superstars of the NEW YORK YANKEES

by Annabelle Tometich

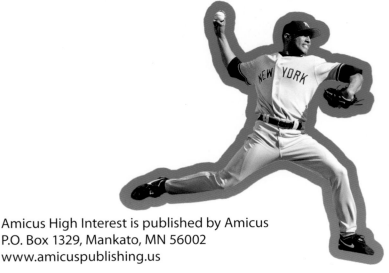

Amicus High Interest is published by Amicus
P.O. Box 1329, Mankato, MN 56002
www.amicuspublishing.us

Library of Congress Cataloging-in-Publication Data
Tometich, Annabelle, 1980-
  Superstars of the New York Yankees / by Annabelle Tometich.
    pages cm. -- (Pro sports superstars)
  Includes index.
  Summary: "Presents some of the New York Yankees' greatest players and
their achievements in pro baseball, including Mariano Rivera and Derek
Jeter"--Provided by publisher.
  ISBN 978-1-60753-594-2 (hardcover) -- ISBN 978-1-60753-628-4 (pdf
ebook)
  1. New York Yankees (Baseball team)--History--Juvenile literature. I. Title.
  GV875.N4T65 2014
  796.357'64097471--dc23
                                        2013044095

Photo Credits: Ron Schwane/AP Images, cover; Elise Amendola/AP
Images, 5; Bettmann/Corbis, 6, 9; AP Images, 10, 13; George Tiedemann/
Corbis, 14; Anthony Correia/Shutterstock Images, 17; Gregory Bull/AP
Images, 18, 22; Kathy Willens/AP Images, 21

Produced for Amicus by The Peterson Publishing Company
and Red Line Editorial.

Editor Arnold Ringstad
Designer Maggie Villaume
Printed in the United States of America
Mankato, MN
2-2014
PA10001
10 9 8 7 6 5 4 3 2 1

TABLE OF CONTENTS

MEET THE NEW YORK YANKEES

The New York Yankees have won 27 **World Series**. No team has won more. The team is more than 100 years old. The Yankees have had many stars. Here are some of the best.

BABE RUTH

Babe Ruth was a powerful hitter. He hit 714 **home runs**. People called him the Sultan of Swat. Ruth helped the team win the 1923 World Series. It was their first.

Babe Ruth started as a pitcher.

LOU GEHRIG

Lou Gehrig worked hard. He played in 2,130 straight games. Gehrig's nickname was The Iron Horse. He helped win six World Series. The last was in 1938.

Two of Joe DiMaggio's brothers also played professional baseball.

JOE DIMAGGIO

Joe DiMaggio is famous for The Streak. It happened in 1941. He had a hit in 56 games in a row. The record still stands. DiMaggio won three **MVP** awards.

MICKEY MANTLE

Mickey Mantle was a great hitter. He won three MVP awards. The first was in 1956. Mantle hit 18 home runs in World Series games. No player has hit more in World Series games.

13

14

REGGIE JACKSON

Reggie Jackson played right field. He helped the Yankees win the 1977 World Series. He hit three home runs in a row in the last game.

MARIANO RIVERA

Mariano Rivera was a **closer**. He has the most **saves** ever. His famous pitch was a cut **fastball**. Rivera won his first World Series in 1996.

Rivera was born in Panama. That is a country in Central America.

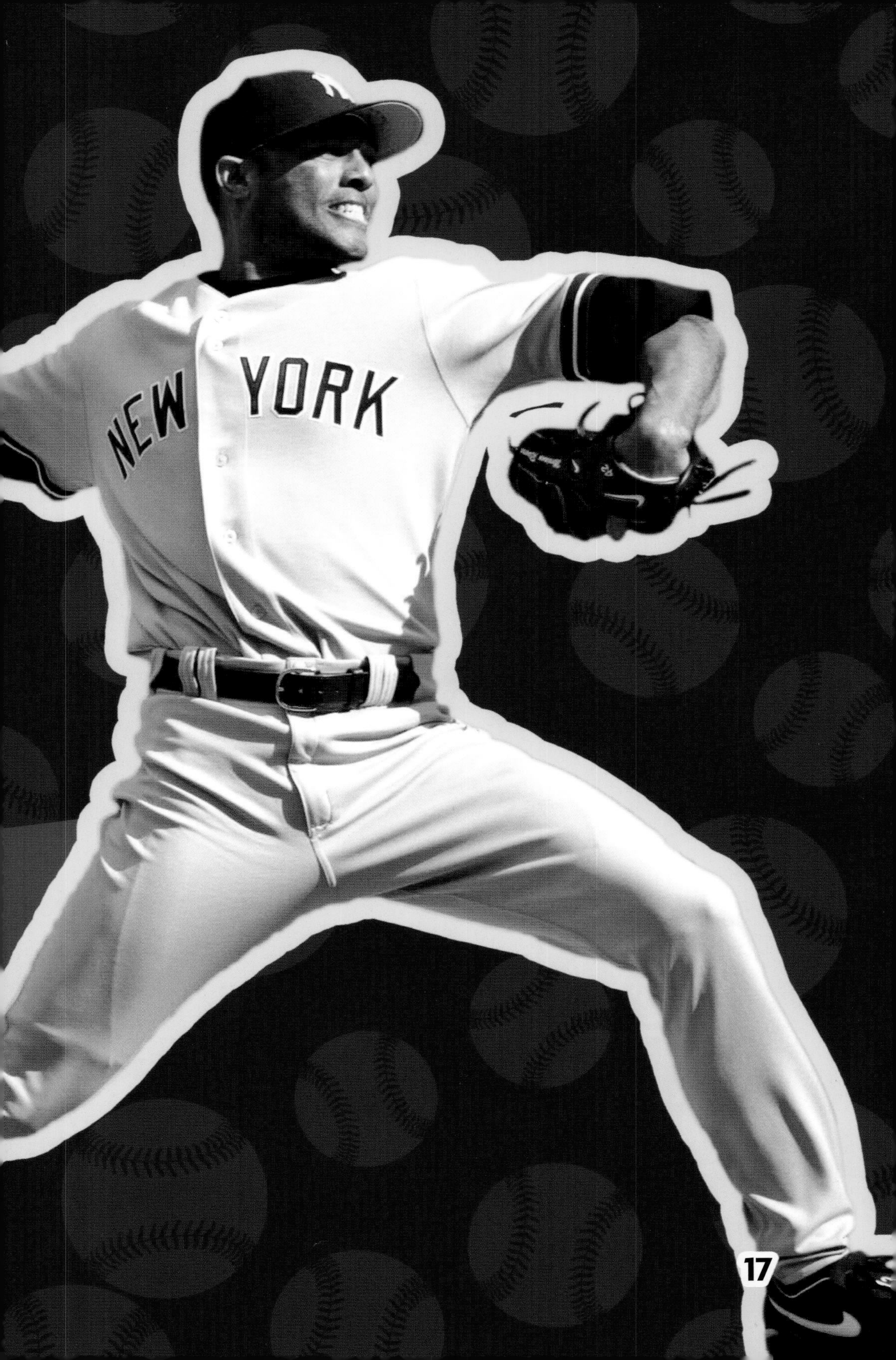
NEW YORK

DEREK JETER

Derek Jeter has been the team **captain** since 2003. He helped the Yankees win five World Series. He also won five **Gold Glove Awards**.

CC SABATHIA

CC Sabathia is a great pitcher. He joined the team in 2009. Sabathia throws accurate pitches. He has struck out more than 2,000 batters.

The Yankees have had many great superstars. Who will be next?

21

TEAM FAST FACTS

Founded: 1901

Other names: Baltimore Orioles (1901-1902), New York Highlanders (1903-1912)

Nicknames: The Bronx Bombers, The Yanks, The Pinstripers

Home Stadium: Yankee Stadium (Bronx, New York)

World Series Championships: 27 (1923, 1927, 1928, 1932, 1936, 1937, 1938, 1939, 1941, 1943, 1947, 1949, 1950, 1951, 1952, 1953, 1956, 1958, 1961, 1962, 1977, 1978, 1996, 1998, 1999, 2000, 2009)

Hall of Fame Players: 34, including Joe DiMaggio, Lou Gehrig, Mickey Mantle, and Babe Ruth

WORDS TO KNOW

captain – a player who leads the team

closer – a player whose main job is to pitch at the end of the game to protect a lead

fastball – a pitch that goes fast and straight

Gold Glove Awards – awards given to the best fielders each year

home runs – hits that go far enough to leave the field, letting the hitter run all the way around the bases to score a run

MVP – Most Valuable Player; an honor given to the best player each season

saves – games won by pitchers who hold a lead at the end of a game

World Series – the annual baseball championship series

LEARN MORE

Books

Christopher, Matt. *The New York Yankees (Legendary Sports Teams)*. New York: Little, Brown, 2009.

Kelley, K. C. *New York Yankees (Favorite Baseball Teams)*. North Mankato, MN: Child's World, 2014.

Web Sites

Baseball History
http://mlb.mlb.com/mlb/history/
Learn more about the history of baseball.

MLB.com
http://mlb.com
See pictures and track your favorite baseball player's stats.

New York Yankees—Official Site
http://newyork.yankees.mlb.com
Watch video clips and read stories about the New York Yankees.

INDEX